New & Selected Poems

A. Alvarez

THE WAYWISER PRESS

LONDON
2002

First published in 2002 by

THE WAYWISER PRESS

9 Woodstock Road, London N4 3ET, UK

T: +44 (0)20 8374 5526
F: +44 (0)20 8374 5736

waywiserpress@aol.com
www.waywiser-press.com

Editor
Philip Hoy

A CIP catalogue record for this book is available from the British Library

ISBN 1-904130-07-0

This book has been published with financial assistance from London Arts

UK Distributor
Orca Book Services, 3 Fleets Lane, Poole, Dorset, BH15 3AJ, UK

N. American Distributor
Dufour Editions Inc., P.O. Box 7, Chester Springs, PA 19425, USA

Printed and Bound by
T.J. International Ltd., Padstow, Cornwall PL28 8RW, UK

to

Anne

Contents

1. New Poems

Anne Dancing 11
Mermaid 12
Blueberries 13
High Dive 15
Night Talk 16
Space Probe 18
Silk 19
Winter Morning 20
The Flowers 21

2. Selected Poems

I. Autumn to Autumn

He Said, She Said 25
Rain 27
Christmas is Coming 28
Snow 29
Summertime 30
Angels in Italy 31
Autumnal 32

II.

Mourning and Melancholia 35
Nature Morte 36
Coming Back 37
War Stories 38
Operation 39

Apparition   41
Back   42
Lovers   43
Spring Fever   44
Lost   45

III.

The Gate   49
Love Affair   50
The Nativity in New Mexico   51
Night Music   52
Anger   53
Waking   54
Autumn Marriage   56
The Hunt   57
Sunstruck   59
The Picture Gallery   60
The Survivor   62

IV.

A Cemetery in New Mexico   65
The Waterfall   67
The Fortunate Fall   68
The Bad Dream and the Photograph   69
The Vigil   70
The Catharsis   71
Closing Time   72
Dying   73

Index of Titles and First lines   75
A Note About the Author   79

1. NEW POEMS

Anne Dancing

You sashay in, twenty years-old again,
Sweatshirt and jeans, eyes closed, a cat-like smile,
Self-satisfied, self-absorbed, hips swaying,
Weaving your intricate steps across
The intricate carpet. The merest glance

At me does it. You're a North American
College girl out on a date, a '50s-style
Dazzler – great legs, cute ass, sweet smile.
        That's Satchmo playing
Your youth back loud and clear. You toss
Your greying, lovely head. You say, "Come on, let's dance."

Mermaid

Supple and slippery above and below,
Sliding wide-eyed under my hands
With a smile like daybreak,

You swim into my life only at night,
Bringing the shush of waves and shingle,
The smell of salt and distance,
The gull cries, the moan of seamarks
And the broken sweep of light
From shrouded promontories.

You ride the storms and calms,
You plunge and surf,
Cruise the depths with sharks and stingrays
And flicker through the feet of children
Paddling in the shallows,

To end up here in the dark between the sheets,
In the gap between dreaming and waking,
Coming ashore with your smile,
Your sea-scent and thrashing tail,
Still slippery from the creation.

Blueberries

It's their plumpness that gets me,
As though they wanted to be something else entirely –
A cherry, an aubergine embryo, a heart
Swollen with love or pride or pleasure –
As though they were bursting out of their skins
With desire and ambition,
With ideas above their station.

And the silvery sheen on their darkness,
A fox fur that bruises easily
Or is licked off like sugar,
Like sweat off a lover.

They colour ice-cream and cordials,
They stud those muffins you love
With bursts of sweetness and stain
The buttery crumbling cake
An imperial purple.

Your favourite fruit, you say.
They remind you of home,
Of summer in Canada,
Of being young and greedy,

Or, older but no less greedy,
Of fields high in the Apennines
Where families were scooping the bushes
With steel combs nailed to wood boxes,
Singing and happy and sweating.
We smelt them before we saw them.

Blueberries have no smell,
But their taste is fragrant and summery.
They taste like flowers would taste
In an edible universe:
A jolt of colour,
Cool skin on the tongue,
Explosions of pleasure.

High Dive

Something happens to your mouth:
The strings go slack around it,
The high wires you balance on when you talk,
Your smile's daredevil trapeze act
And its glittering arcs
Are still as night.

The audience goes dumb.
A single drum
Beats softly in expectation.
You poise there, looking down,
Then, inch by inch,
Slowly raise your head,
Breathe out, breathe in,
Then plunge.

Night Talk

In the dream you were leaning forward,
In a gauzy top with a rose,
Your breasts hanging clear of the fabric,
A fresh-minted Eve in her garden,
Raw colour among the foliage,
Forked lightning against starlight,
Jolting me awake.

Leaning forward as if to say,
What more do you want? Come on.
There's nothing to get in the way
Of palm and sweating palm,
Moist lip and inner lip,
Eyelash on delicate eyelash,
Inquisitive fingertip,
Breath mingling with breath
And not a hair's breadth between,
Nothing between us but shadows,
A few shreds of gossamer,
A tattered woven rose.

I woke to the thud of my heart,
Tangled hair and tangled sheets,
Tick of the bedside clock,
You muttering in your sleep
Something I couldn't make out.

Dear sleeper haunting my dreams,
Was it me you were you talking to?
We might as well be one
Person tricked out as two
'Til death us do part. Dream on,
Just turn my way while you sleep,
World without end. Amen.

Space Probe

Head back, eyes closed, dazed smile.
You're gone again,
Off to some other planet,
Down a black hole.
So long. Nice knowing you. Take care.

There should be tolling bells,
The moan and clang of buoys,
Trains whistling in the dark
And heart-sick long farewells.
Not "Hey!" and "Gosh!" and "Jeez!"
That's schoolgirl talk.

Is that where you've gone?
The back of the family Ford?
The drive-in? The Senior Prom?
Or galloping through the trees with your handsome dad?

You're everywhere. You're nowhere.
You're home. Remember me?
The guy who waved you goodbye welcomes you back,
Opens the curtains, turns off the light.
Did it go all right wherever it is you have been?
I know how it all goes wrong,
So where did it all go right?

Silk

White, I thought, white
Silk at your throat.
I was wrong.

A faint infusion of pink:
Blood under the skin,
Spring under the snow,
Wine tainting the milk.

Now I no longer know
Which I want more:
To run my hand over the silk
Or over the skin below.

Winter Morning

Watching you move, with the hair over your face,
Your square shoulders and flexible back,
And your con-trail of Kleenex,

Watching your long dancer's legs coming and going
In the slit of your night dress
And your painted toenails
Coming and going beneath,

Catching the faint, urgent scent
Of the space between your breasts
And the musk between your thighs,
I wake up grudgingly.

Slit-eyed, bad-tempered, full of sleep,
Needing the bathroom, needing a cup of tea,
You close the window on the freezing street
And head for the door. Then stop and raise
A hand as though in blessing:

"Hi," you say. "Hi." Your drop-dead smile
Shimmers, another con-trail, when you're gone.

The Flowers

You see them across rooms,
Long-stemmed and delicate,
Nodding their shining heads
In the stir and gossip,
Shooting the breeze.

Close up's more perilous. They have
A danger zone of fragrance
And the colours are subtler:
Slow smile of recognition,
Eyes brightening and darkening,
Nervous fingers holding you transfixed.

Each to its season, blooming, fading:
Outrageous snowdrops and crocuses
Piercing the dank soil; mayflower
With its contagious clouds of scent;
Summer's prodigal blaze;
Then the slow glowing isolated
Fires of winter roses.

Beauty takes courage. Courage itself
Is beautiful. Erect and steady
In snow and darkness, my darling,
Keep faith. Wait for the spring.

2. Selected Poems

I. Autumn to Autumn

September 1974 – September 1975

He Said, She Said

Abruptly, the smell of flowers, sharp, far, delicate,
The old heart beating sweetly, eyes
Fresh as an apple, all the wrinkles gone.
Who would have thought it? Not her, not him.

Something passed through the room and didn't linger.
"Did you see its face?" she said. He said,
"What was it saying?" "'Gone',"
She replied, "Or that's what I thought it said."
He answered, "Not so. 'Come', I'm sure it was 'come'.
It beckoned," he said. "We should follow. It won't come back."
"Hawthorn in autumn," she said. "Don't make me laugh.
'Gone' was the word, and it's gone. Don't be a fool."

"Hawthorn," he said, "mayflower, the late smell of spring.
Everything's opening up, just like it was.
Won't you come with me?" he said. "We've still
Got a chance. Listen. Smell it," he said.
"We've been reprieved." Slowly, idly,
She shook her heavy head and turned away.
"I won't be waiting," she said. "Don't think I will."

The hair dark round her face, her eyes shrouded.
"Never," she said. "I've waited enough already."
He answered, "Listen. It's calling. It's our last chance."
Like food, like rain, like mist. Mouth open, heart open.

"All that blossom," he said, "like when we were young."
"When *were* we young?" she asked. "I don't remember."

A flicker of gold, a smile, a far voice calling
Confusedly, "Come," "Gone," "Come." The jumbled scents
Of spring on the autumn night. "Our last chance," he said.
And she answered, "You take it without me."

Rain

New leaf, new world, the rain comes down.
A shimmering figure in red, who is it? Who?
Wine-red, a halo of light, a faint clean scent,
Lips parted, attentive, the clear eyes wide
And smiling: "This is the end of the road.

Begin again." Again, again, the echo fading.
Listen. The rain comes pattering down, a small
Persistent sound, heaping and falling like sand.
Time is running out. Why won't you listen?
Quiet. Cars hiss in the street, the rain comes down.

"Never again," says the voice. Like a fan opening
Slowly, slowly the light brightens then fades,
The fan closing, the night shuts in again.

New leaf, new heart, old love, the world
Turns us its morning face, smooth after sex,
Softened, tranquil with sleep. It eyes us gravely.
"Time to begin," it says. "Time to begin."

Christmas is Coming

The imagination may be compared to Adam's dream – he awoke and found it truth. – Keats

A blue sky smeared with grey, the gulls
Swimming in light. Clear after storm.
Air still, the branches still and broken.
Forests dip in the sea, the smoke curls blue
Against the blue. A flattened, sleeping ocean.

Below the horizon thunder. What does it matter?
Everything seeps away, even the storm.
The day darkens at four, the blue turns ink.
Then night, starless and chill. Then the folds of sleep.

Hull down on the horizon the dream yacht rides.
Slim, white as a tusk, sleek and smooth,
Billowing clouds of sail. Look at her move.
Hiss and creak in the silence. The eye of God
Watches her. Look at her move. He's satisfied.
Look at her move into waking, closer, closer,
Pulling clear of the dream, coming to land.

Morning. Morning again. The children are singing
Lustily and off-key, announcing the holiday,
A new life coming, a bare and shadowless world
And the tender blue of the sky. The yacht is docked.
Nobody stirs, nobody speaks. They wait
For the cargo of toys, cake, fruit, the unthinkable
Seasonal pleasures. Silence. A spar
Creaks. Silence. Then from the cabin
Laughter. Quietly laughing
The serene dream head rises into day.

Snow

Elsewhere the snow comes down, all the dead whiteness.
I am warm in front of the fire, warm and unquiet.
Malignant the weight in the chest's cave, stirring, stirring.
The logs flicker and smoke, the dim light jumps.
Life. The snow falls blankly. Crack and hiss
Of the fire. To the flower-faced clock my heart
Stubbornly echoes, "What's this? What's this? What's this?"

It is larger than it seems. It overflows
Your curves and slopes, your secret tastes and textures,
The delicate planes of shoulder, thigh and cheek.
Its blues and whites are clear as day, but deep.
Rivers run through it, moons tilt, watery suns,
Creatures move stealthily under its glimmering skin.
A new world swarming, swarming. Let me in.

You blush and hang your head, shuffle your feet
And hesitate. Love, be patient and still.
Already the wind is turning, spring patrols the street,
The first buds stir under the snow on the hill.

Summertime

Frail greens and ragged petals blown about
Mindlessly. The tree nudges me, dipping and reaching.
Absence and the lost voices. Nudged by the trees.
Wing-beats. What are they saying, leaf to leaf?
The swallows high, the thick clouds coming and going
About their business. Where do I go? The leaves
Like surf hissing far off. They keep to themselves.
Spring and its chills have receded, a hot sun rides
The fuming clouds day after day after day.

They keep to themselves, are numb, are going nowhere
Day after day after day. A faint sea-murmur
Coming and going, rising and falling. Lost.
Don't know the language. Can't make out the names.
Absence. Frail greens and floating petals and light
Clear as a note of music, pure and clear.
The privet smelling green, its green-white flowers
Pungent, like urine. Shadows taking over
A dry, thin world. The trees dip to the wind, their leaves
Seethe in the spiral of summer, saying, Beware.
Saying, Too late. Saying, Too brief. Saying, It's gone.

Angels in Italy

They make no noise, though their wings move,
Pale white against pale blue, upwards and slow,
Watching us, curious, clear eyes, clear foreheads,
Hair streaming away behind, sun in sun,
Till the flank of the mountain hides them.
Chestnut, spruce, scrub oak and fir
Tangling up to the ridge. Then blue, blue, blue.

Such solitude. Calm faces, falling hair,
Poised wings and sinewy pinions. The clouds
Have them now. Soaring, circling. Gone away.
Leaving the murmur of water, vine leaves saying, "Shush,"
Leaves of the walnut rattling like dice.

A car rasps in the valley. Someone is cutting
Wood with a buzz-saw, harsh, not letting go.
Now come the children, the wives, the gossip and cooking,
Evening and thickening light. A brisk wind sweeps
From ridge to ridge bringing silence.
Each of us pauses, absent, lost in himself,
Stilled by the sound of the river.

A glint of white against blue.
"Clouds," you say, "clouds."
No, wings. Listen. Wings heavily beating,
Rustle of feathers, shoulders flexing smoothly
Beyond the ridge. But I answer,
"Clouds, yes, clouds.
Tomorrow, love, tomorrow there'll be rain."

Autumnal

Light. The colours are changing. Light
Seeps through the leaves, thin clouds, thin air,
Thin blood and distance, always distance.

Is this what it means to get old? Thinness and space,
Everything leaking away. The heavy trees
Are shedding, shedding their wealth:
Russet and gold in the green and glints of flame.

They scatter themselves with both hands, prodigally,
Careless, the last big spenders. Like heads of hair
The willows bend to the pond, and toss and sway.

Clouds bank high in the east, a sharp wind veers.
There's a cold time coming, my dear. The trees
Unravel their summer stuff, whispering, "Who
Gives a damn, gives a damn, gives a damn?"
Light-headed, becoming lighter, their minds elsewhere.

Above us a peregrine, curved and tense as a blade,
Glides on the wind and waits.
The beautiful spaces are his, the variegated
Trees and darkening fields diminishing
Below him, the chill greys shifting above.
A kingdom, empty and loveless. What do we have?
We have the inner spaces, darkening, growing,
Like an eye dilating with fear, like a heart giving up.

II.

Mourning and Melancholia

His face was blue, on his fingers
Flecks of green. "This is my father,"
I thought. Stiff and unwieldy
He stared out of my sleep. The parlourmaid
Smiled from the bed with his corpse,
Her chapped lips thin and welcoming.
In the next room her albino child
Kept shouting, shouting. I had to put him down
Like a blind puppy. "Death from strangulation
By persons known." I keep the clipping
In my breast-pocket where it burns and burns,
Stuck to my skin like phosphorus.

I wake up struggling, silent; undersea
Light and a single thrush
Is tuning up. You sleep, the baby sleeps,
The town is dead. Foxes are out on the Heath;
They sniff the air like knives.
A hawk turns slowly over Highgate, waiting.
This is the hidden life of London. Wild.

Three years back my father's corpse was burnt,
His ashes scattered. Now I breathe him in
With the grey morning air, in and out.
In out. My heart bumps steadily
Without pleasure. The air is thick with ash.
In out. I am cold and powerless. His face
Still pushes sadly into mine. He's disappointed.
I've let him down, he says. Now I'm cold like him.
Cold and untameable. Will have to be put down.

Nature Morte

Gale in the narrow streets. Wet shadows heaving.
The traffic a broken voice, a failing heart.
The leaves peel off like secrets. Streetlights shiver
Excitedly. My steps don't make a sound.

A still life framed in a window. The dark wood
Glows. Lamplight and firelight.
Rugs soak up the amber, a clock beats,
Beats. No one's about. No one's a– Only the wind.

And a girl's face in a silver frame on a stranger's table.
As strange as my own youth. Beautiful mouth,
A smile and a blur of trouble. I can't remember
The names, the breasts, the scents, or the man who sought them.

The face in the frame is radiant. It smiles at me
Across the silent room, into the night,
Glowing and unconcerned. What was I doing?
It fades. What have I done? What have I lost?

Coming Back

Finer and clearer than the mountain air
Or the wheeling New Mexican sun.
Your scent in the back of my mind like a cry from another street.
Something uncoils and breathes. Night moves
With the musky taste of summer. Turn and sleep.
Your eyes change in the firelight. You have changed.

Love, the weather has turned, the swallows are back
And I wake in your scattered hair sensing rain
Where the trees arch over our bed.
Their thin leaves rustle your name.

War Stories

The first time they all looked shocked.
"Don't tell such filthy stories
around here," they said. "How dare you?"
And everyone snickered.

The second time they shook a little
and there was a booming
something like laughter. As the dust rose
he found himself crying.

The third time he brought the house down.
They rolled in the aisles and the aisles rolled.
"That's marvellous," they cried, tears streaming down their faces,
"Oh, do stop." And blew him to pieces.

Operation

The town froze, close as a fist.
Winter was setting about us.
Like birds the bare trees shivered,
Birds without leaves or nests
As the fog took over.

My words were all gone, my tongue sour.
We sat in the car like the dead
Awaiting the dead. Your hair
Wept round your face like a willow
Unstirring. Your eyes were dry.

Unbodied, like smoke in the crowd,
You vanished. Later came violence.
Not that you felt it or cared,
Swaddled in drugs, apart
In some fractured, offensive dream,
While a bog-Irish nurse mopped up.

"Leave me. I'm bleeding. I'm still
Bleeding. But he didn't hurt me."
Pale as the dead. As the dead
Fragile. Vague as the city
Now the fog chokes down again.
A life was pitched out like garbage.

"I'm bleeding. A boy, they said."
My blood stings like a river
Lurching over the falls.
My hands are bloody. My mind

Is rinsed with it. Blood fails me.
You lie like the dead, still bleeding,
While his fingers, unformed, unerring,
Hold us and pick us to pieces.

Apparition

"Beaver. Beaver," you whisper,
"Beaver," yearningly.
A wetness glimmers,
Sleek fur, teeth sly,
Cold paw at your throat,
Cold eye to your eye.
Cold cold cold.
"Help me," you sigh,
Shoulder bloody, breasts straining
To the shuddering, stained sky.

Back

The night I came back from the hospital, scarcely
Knowing what had happened or when,
I went through the whole performance again in my dreams.
Three times – in a dance, in a chase and in something
Now lost – my body was seized and shaken
Till my jaw swung loose, my eyes were almost out
And my trunk was stunned and stretched with a vibration
Sharper than fear, closer than pain. It was death.
So I sweated under the sheets, afraid to sleep,
Though you breathed all night quietly enough by my side.

Was it the *tremor mortis*, the last dissolution
Known now in dreams, unknown in the pit itself
When I was gripped by the neck till my life shook
Like loosening teeth in my head? Yet I recall
Nothing of death but the puzzled look on your face,
Swimming towards me, weeping, clouded, uncertain,
As they took the tube from my arm
And plugged the strange world back in place.

Lovers

Eres como la rosa
De Alejandria:
Colorada de noche,
Blanca de día.

White by day coloured by night
Vivid watching changing white
As lightning by day by night
Seeping colours corrupting cheek wrist hand
As blood runs as fire trembles as green
Water flickers or a bland
Glass block shatters rainbows between
My eye and the fused sunlight

By night coloured by day white

Spring Fever

Too young to know
And far too young to care
What shapes hover
At the head of the stair,

You twist your hands,
Your hair falls round your face
Darkly. The fire breeds shadows.
I keep my place

Although the rain wakes
And the blackbirds call
Fluently, fluently
The leaves uncurl

On wet apple trees.
You stretch your arms
Pleased with your body's
Fluent warmth.
But your eyes stay down.

Be wakeful. Be gentle.
Look, the dark gathers
Inside your head.
It tangles your fingers.
Your wrists fill with blood.

Be gentle. Be wakeful.
From the fire to the shadows
At the top of the stairs
Come to bed.

Lost

My sleep falters and the good dreams:
The sky lit green, you reaching, reaching out
Through a bell of air. I stir.

The same wrist lies along my cheek.
My fingers touch it. The same head on my chest
Stirs. My arms round the same body.
And I feel the dead arms stir.
My fingers in the same dead hair.
The same belly, dead thighs stir.

The dream whirs, cuts. The day blinks, stirs.
Hers. Not yours, my love. Hers.

III.

The Gate

I knew she stood at the gate
And I should swing over towards her
And open the gate on the flood
And the field running down to the water.

But I couldn't. The water ran on,
She went about her work
Wistful, puzzled, dark.
When I opened the gate she had gone.

The fields have dried out and the sun
Has shattered their surface like glass.
Splintered, silvered, down
Lies the gate I couldn't cross.

"Come to me later, elsewhere."
Like rain her voice sighs in the pines.
"Elk range our pastures here,
Bobcat, bear and porcupine."

Love Affair

The sun sees many flowers, but the flower sees only the sun:
Blinded three parts of the day, or dark all dark,
Uneasy, cold, attentive for release,
He crouches through the night, or burns and swells
Blindly as in a kind of hurt of love.
They call it blossoming. The unwieldy earth
Clamps round, his sap distrained and petals shrunk.

And nothing is said. The sun moves on above,
Indifferent, raging in its own sweet fire
And light, light, light, the flower twists for it,
Straining its mouth for death, which it calls love.
"A god has come upon me," gapes the flower
As over the lip of the earth the sun sinks down.
The moon swings to and fro between the trees
Its casual, icy face. The first leaves fall.

The Nativity in New Mexico

Heaving, as though nailed down, and weak with fear
She lay staring at the window pane,
Past vacant yard, past *ponderoso*, where
The desert rolled beneath the mounting sun.

Moaned and turned over. Through the empty air
Sent out her breath towards the breathless plain
In one long, sliding, fading heave of terror.
She heard her husband stir in the next room.

Let him. The blank wind moved across the yard,
The needles of the pine lifted and fell
Against the fiery morning. And she heard
Out of the fire the grating voices call.

So. So. Now her time has passed she strains to see
The grinning midwife lift on high, heels first,
The child, inverted, crying gratingly.
Her thighs are sticky with the afterbirth.

Night Music

It started as a sound deep in your throat,
Guttural, needy, blind as though with pain,
A song not sung for me. You sing yourself:
A voice thrown over voices, a wish calling
Out of the body's pit, till the god emerges
Unhurried. Dark behind him floats his hair.

He moves as wave on wave; between them, stillness.
Infirm as water, steady as the tide,
Your voice runs too and sleep runs underneath.

The god of the house stands at the foot of our bed,
A thickening of darkness against the unsteady shadows,
And makes no sign. He would not stir a feather
Although the wind runs wild in the trees outside.

So, as I sleep, you watch. You change my dreams
With weeping in the dark till sleep becomes
Uneasy, dry and eerie as your song.

Anger

They go at each other like wolves hunting in winter
In a land made thin and savage by the cold.
Is it the season sets one at the other,
    Where once the forest was love?

Is it the season edges them together
Violent and raw as nerves? Now tooth and pelt
Rasp into life as flint upon a tinder,
    Yet once the substance was love.

Now they have done with sidling from thicket to thicket.
The forest knots like a storm about their heads
And a wind poises evilly in the blackness
    Which once was easy with love.

They twist apart, stopped short by their hearts' thick violence.
The starved, hard, anguished landscape lets them in,
Two dwindling backs gone grey and thin with distance
    Where once was the forest of love.

Waking

A train was crying as the dawn came up,
Uncanny, unreal, greyish. The birds began,
Before the humans the birds were harshly twittering,
Crying on all sides, rustling and peopling the air
With outcry, like a river suddenly heard,
A heavy, persistent down-calling. So the birds
Were shaking their song out, wrenching and spilling it
Out of the roots of the heart painfully singing.

Out of the roots of the heart painfully twisting
The cold comes blank as the dawn over our bed
Where you lie with your body away, your face to the wall.
Should I get up, go out and leave you asleep
Before the business of the day has taken us?
Creak down the stairs and out? But to what purpose?
The birds will lose their song in the dull street,
The lorries roll and life goes out of us.

Dying. With so much hate behind the tongue,
The nerves grate but the mouth rests surly and slow,
And action turns on itself A door bangs shut
And God knows now who in the shadow lurks.
My stomach twists to see your passive hands,
Your tensed and quiet forehead, beating throat.
But much good it would do to be up and quit of the lot.

For the beautiful summer is lost and lost the birds,
The lucid, moving air, the swaying elms
And all the confusing paraphernalia of love.
We are left to ourselves in our grey untender rooms,

Sleeping the nights apart in the same bed,
Divided by fears and loss and ignorance.
The dawn comes up and the birds sing to themselves.

Autumn Marriage

WIFE: The year is moving out and I too turn
To noise and colour ...

HUSBAND: Fictions. Here at home
Marriage breeds silence round us and between.

WIFE: There's something else I need, something you lack
To split my fabric open to the heart.

HUSBAND: "They have it very oft that have it not."

WIFE: Domestic weather, violent and void,
Clouds us from the kitchen to the bed.

HUSBAND: Who would have dreamed the sky could turn so black?

WIFE: This summer sickens me, this harvest calm
Without fruition strips me to the bone.
My heart curls like a leaf, my sap is down.

HUSBAND: Then wait for the colder season, glassy dawns,
Frost shapes on the window, rime on the lawn,
The birds piping chill from the gun-blue stones.
Then, despite blankets, hot-water bottle, stove,
The heart contracts its kingdom and you'll move
Back toward me for warmth ...

WIFE: If not for love.

The Hunt

The air is dry as salt, the desert ribbed
Between scrub and heat and mountain.
The sun bakes like an eye in a blank face,
Or, delicate as a mother, swells the moon.

By night the stars are touchable as fruit
About the hut. The undergrowth is quick
With hidden life. Deer tread the cooling fields
Like ghosts, and shrill as ghosts the swaying bats.

And so I hunt by night. I see with my feet
Among the piñon, along vague, straggling tracks
Up from the cabin, through the breathing forest,
Moving by moonlight. Silence. Patience. Stealth.

A tentative sound begins: a woman talking
Raptly, excitedly murmuring to herself?
The mountain stream runs thin as breath through its shallows.
I follow the woman's voice to its dammed-up source

Where logs are tangled thick and silt builds up,
Where water flickers fragile and loose as light
And something hesitates: a shadow drinks at the clearness,
Insubstantial, takes substance like food from a cup.

I gather, silent and poised among the bushes.
(Life of my life, flesh of my flesh) I aim
And (with my body I thee worship) fire.
The creature rises, arches, flays the pool,

Its legs as taut as needles, its head wild.
It leaps like a cry on the air, is torn inside
And gives out its life to the watery silt and the moon.
Shapeless. Jerking. Loveless. Without pride.

Slowly the noise dies away. The heart's crashing
Fades up the mountain and settles, too, the shocked
Whisper and rustle of beasts who have seen the slaying.
The creature trembles. It is my own blood spurts.

Sunstruck

My eyes swayed, I curved
As though kicked in the groin.
And you were full of it, thick with the sun.
In your delicate, reeking skin,
Swollen, tasting of brine,
Those shuttered afternoons:
Feet bare on the tiles, the muffled sounds
Outside and muffled, hissing within
The rustle of love. Light in bars. A thin
Crying. High up. Held up. Sliding. Sliding. Gone.
You came back full of it,
Wanting another man's child.
Sick to the bone, the vein, the groin.
Thick with the sun.

The Picture Gallery

The voices fade and steps, as dry as air ...
Where do you lie now? Under what shifting trees?
Under whose shifting hands? ... Startled the images
As rain drifts round the eaves,
Each in its own gold frame. Pain hangs on the walls,
Sifts like dust from the palms
While the spiked head, watching, lolls.

Even the mother and child are tense with waiting;
They stare from the wall with the same aching eyes.

The mother twines with the child. The frame empties ...
Under whose hands you lie, under whose ... Streets
Flicker with lights, with fragments twisted together ...
Thrusting, the hands with hands twine, feet with feet ...

Pain in the brick, in asphalt as in marble,
Turning the earth in spring like a heel grinds down,
Wrenches the vivid beak of a whistling blackbird
Whose eye is sharp as a knife among the leaves,
Hovers, pounces, tears, and does not breed ...
You lie against him listlessly for hours.
Your breathing is an ache, your sex a bruise ...

It wakes with the restless child turning at midnight,
Leans at the foot of the bed attentive at dawn ...
Who stirs? Who moves a hand along your spine? ...
Starts from the lights as traffic nudges forward,
Sways through the park where lovers flicker and weave ...
And in your mouth whispers obscenities ...

And to the crowd at some nervous rustling meeting
Grates through the speaker's teeth when trouble starts.
Pain has invaded the city and gapes at its heart.

And you, under whose hands now five years gone
In the same room in the same restless dawn
I lay, now lie under whose hands, whose thighs,
And stare at the wall with the same aching eyes?

The Survivor

The skull in my hands is my life's. It stares at me.
My child peers out through its eyes, my wife's lips move
Across the polished bone where its lips should be.
Her hair is soft on the crown and burns for love.

We are held in a single death: child, husband, wife,
Mixed blood, mixed feelings, fingers mixed and minds
Burn in a single flame across our lives,
And I am left with a delicate skull in my hands.

Strange that a bone should flame as though dipped in pitch,
Strangely intense in death, strange tenderness
In blood that once leapt to a cheek now cold to my touch.
Death clasps them bone to bone against his chest.

Only the skull is left, the last hard fact
That turns in my hands, in my blood, under my skin,
Pacing my life like a traveller who taps
The earth and cries, "Dear mother, let me in."

IV.

d even here in this clear afternoon
e dead are moving like wind among the pines;
ey touch my mouth, they curl along my spine.
ey are waiting for me. Why won't they call my name?

A Cemetery in New Mexico

To Alfred Alvarez, died 1957

Softly the dead stir, call, through the afternoo
The soil lies too light upon them and the win
Blows through the earth as though the earth v

Ar
Th
Th
Th

My own blood in a heavy northern death
Sleeps with the rain and clay and dark, thick s
Where the spirit fights for movement as for br

But among these pines the crosses grow like f(
Frail sprouting wood and mottled, slender stor
And the wind moves, through shadows moves

Delicate the light, the air, a breathing
Joins mourners to the dead in one light sleep:
I watch as I would watch a blind man sleeping,

And remember the day the creaking ropes let s
My grandfather's heavy body into his grave,
And the rain came down as we shovelled the ear

The clods fell final and flat as a blow in the win
While the mourners patiently hunched against t
There were Hebrew prayers I didn't understand.

In Willesden Cemetery, honoured, wealthy, pro
Unyielding and remote, he bides his time.
And carved above his head is my own name.

Over and over again the thing begins:
My son at night now frets us with his cries
When dark above his crib the same face leans.

The Waterfall

In the soft afternoon air my soft afternoon neighbour
Starts screaming from the belly of his throat.
Only before of cars, his daughters, liquor,
Now he is yelling his head off with a voice
Like night, like nightmare: "No. No. No. No. No."

No more. The soft street sways with the explosion.
The sun survives the clouds. Birds reassume
Their privileges. The traffic mumbles on
Like sleep. No tears, no explanations.
Only that voice from behind the sheet of the waterfall,
The lost thing from the cave with a mouth like a navel:
"NO."

Under the skein of the street its echoes flow.

The Fortunate Fall

Perhaps Eve in the garden knew the sun
With her whole flesh, and pruned the rose's soul –
The thing was thornless, pliable, like Eve –
And she the garden whence all flowers sprung.

But Adam knew her as the fruit he stole,
The apple, sleeping, God made him conceive.
His side and eyes were opened. They were bare,
The tree despoiled and knowledge risen whole.

Before she even fumbled with the leaves
Adam was finished. Of course, she had a flair
For fumbling that was folly to oppose –
Tricky, pleading, knowing. Why should he grieve?

So he chose for her, chose his own despair.
Her hair, like rain, closed on the thorny rose.

The Bad Dream and the Photograph

Even in sleep your shadow watches me.
Your whisper rustles through the sleeping room
As though you moved in silks. Why keep on trying?
Nothing can turn you full-face to the noon.

I fool myself with pains you cannot feel.
You are contorted on another wheel.

It is some illness haunts you. Thin as water,
Your cry draws out my pain and breath in one.
The whole thing flickers to a halt. You fade
And I perhaps might gape to find you gone.

But only stir and know you will not sleep,
Gazing obliquely through the chilly dawn.
For what? Your uneasy trance will never break,
Your smiling never save you from the dark,
Nor I, for knowing you, be less alone.

The Vigil

The spider love that transubstantiates all – Donne

You stand in the first dumbness of the snow
As finely, the gauze drop in pantomime,
All detail fades upon your startled face
And back to darkness line and colour flow.

The final trance and rapture of the bone
Has come. What rain on stone and age in us
Raddle, the snow dispenses equally –
Years towards death in one short afternoon.

The mouth lifts at one corner, on the crown
Regally twists the hair against the white
Stark imposition of a nervous fit,
Ageing in frozen tumult like a clown.

You mime stock-still your final comic pose:
Seduced by the earthy widower of spades
Slowly to dissolution and the blank
Tumbler's lust for stature and repose.

The Catharsis

It is the tenderness you feel you know
You may have had the tenderness you miss.

Still in the mask you wear your tongue can go
Raptly to themes the audience won't guess

Creating from those fragments of thin air
Within the head's 0 what you might have been.

You are not less because they cannot share
All that you are and tell what they have seen.

Yet they're agog. Your eloquence will flow
Beyond the measure pacing your distress

Till it breaks down the limits of your care
And finally you relish what you seem

And are to your last sense all you forgo:
Love. The particular. No more no less.

Closing Time

Day drains, the colours harden and stare, thin leaves
Chatter, unnatural space between trees.
Something is missing. Go, says the thrush, let it be.

Crows in the damp air bicker, gulls go over.
Unpredictable the skeletons of trees,
Unlike ours. But ominous like ours.

Red mud, trickle of water, floating weeds.
Small birds hiding, flickering from the light.
What are they frightened of? You, says the owl, you, you.

The keepers are closing the woods, ringing bells
And shouting, "Everyone out. Everyone out."
Boots on the sodden paths, brass tongues licking brass.

Light shrinks, the frost takes hold. Voices, voices
Among the bushes, shades muttering together
About old times. Damp breath, extinguished eyes.

I turn my back and go. Houses, lights,
The lake where ducks are gossiping comfortably
And traffic mumbles homeward, homeward to sleep.

It's a winter evening. I miss you. Wish you were here.
"Everyone out," comes the answer. "Everyone out."

Dying

Death is before me today
    like recovering from an illness
    and going into the garden

Death
    the odour of myrrh
    a sail's curving shadow on a windy day

Death
    like the scent of the lotus
    like lingering on the shore of drunkenness

Death
    a quick, cool stream
    a soldier coming home

Death
    like a break in the clouds
    a bird's flight into the unknown

Death
    like homesickness
    like homecoming after captivity.

Adapted from a translation
from the Ancient Egyptian

Index of Titles and First Lines

A blue sky smeared with grey, the gulls   28
A Cemetery in New Mexico   65
A train was crying as the dawn came up   54
Abruptly, the smell of flowers, sharp, far, delicate   25
Angels in Italy   31
Anger   53
Anne Dancing   11
Apparition   41
Autumn Marriage   56
Autumnal   32
Back   42
"Beaver. Beaver," you whisper   41
Blueberries   13
Christmas is Coming   28
Closing Time   72
Coming Back   37
Day drains, the colours harden and stare, thin leaves   72
Death is before me today   73
Dying   73
Elsewhere the snow comes down, all the dead whiteness   29
Even in sleep your shadow watches me   69
Finer and clearer than the mountain air   37
Frail greens and ragged petals blown about   30
Gale in the narrow streets. Wet shadows heaving   36
He Said, She Said   25
Head back, eyes closed, dazed smile   18
Heaving, as though nailed down, and weak with fear   51
High Dive   15
His face was blue, on his fingers   35
I knew she stood at the gate   49
In the dream you were leaning forward   16
In the soft afternoon air my soft afternoon neighbour   67
It is the tenderness you feel you know   71
It started as a sound deep in your throat   52
It's their plumpness that gets me   13
Light. The colours are changing. Light   32

Lost	45
Love Affair	50
Lovers	43
Mermaid	12
Mourning and Melancholia	35
My eyes swayed, I curved	59
My sleep falters and the good dreams	45
Nature Morte	36
New leaf, new world, the rain comes down	27
Night Music	52
Night Talk	16
Operation	39
Perhaps Eve in the garden knew the sun	68
Rain	27
Silk	19
Snow	29
Softly the dead stir, call, through the afternoon	65
Something happens to your mouth	15
Space Probe	18
Spring Fever	44
Summertime	30
Sunstruck	59
Supple and slippery above and below	12
The air is dry as salt, the desert ribbed	57
The Bad Dream and the Photograph	69
The Catharsis	71
The first time they all looked shocked	38
The Flowers	21
The Fortunate Fall	68
The Gate	49
The Hunt	57
The Nativity in New Mexico	51
The night I came back from the hospital, scarcely	42
The Picture Gallery	60
The skull in my hands is my life's. It stares at me	62
The sun sees many flowers, but the flowers see only the sun	50
The Survivor	62
The town froze, close as a fist	39
The Vigil	70
The voices fade and steps, as dry as air ...	60
The Waterfall	67

The year is moving out and I too turn   56
They go at each other like wolves hunting in winter   53
They make no noise, though their wings move   31
Too young to know   44
WAKING   54
WAR STORIES   38
Watching you move, with the hair over your face   20
White by day coloured by night   43
White, I thought, white   19
WINTER MORNING   20
You sashay in, twenty years-old again   11
You see them across rooms   21
You stand in the first dumbness of the snow   70

A Note About The Author

Al Alvarez is a poet, novelist, literary critic, anthologist, and author of many non-fiction books on topics ranging from suicide, divorce and dreams – *The Savage God, Life After Marriage, Night* – to poker, North Sea oil and mountaineering – *The Biggest Game in Town, Offshore, Feeding the Rat.* His most recent books are an autobiography, *Where Did It All Go Right?* and *Poker: Bets, Bluffs, and Bad Beats.* He lives in London.